THE GREAT ARTISTS

Van Gogh

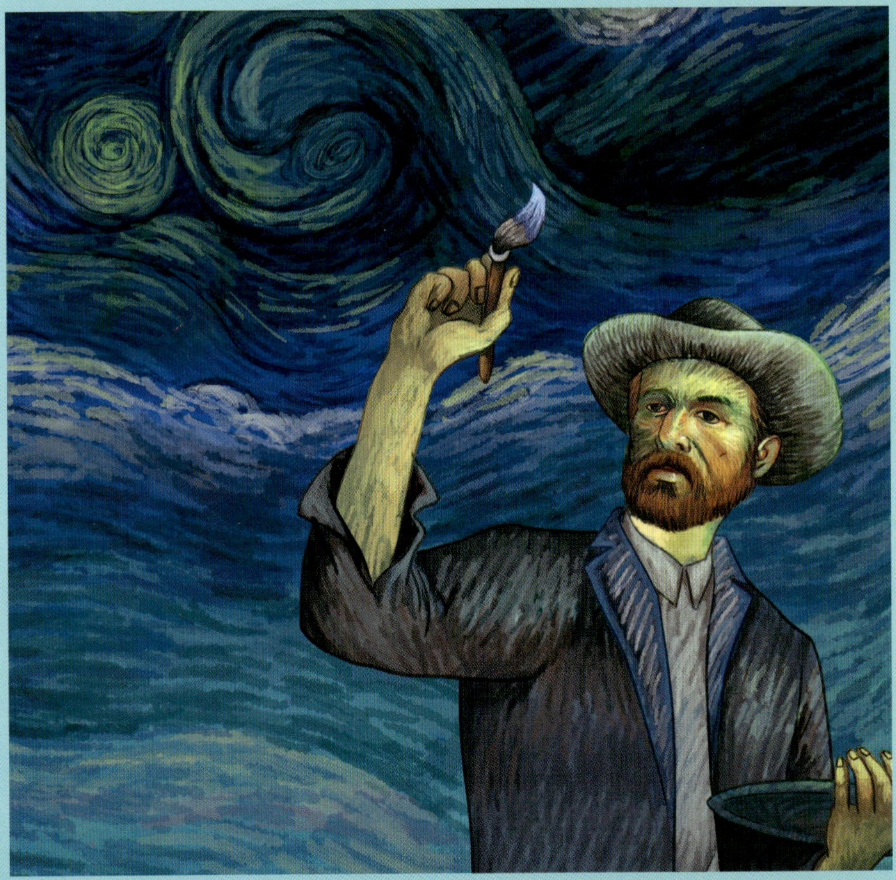

Om KIDZ

An imprint of Om Books International

Vincent Willem van Gogh was born on 30 March, 1853, in Groot Zundert, a village in the Netherlands. His father was a strict parish minister and his mother, who was very strong willed, had an interest in botany and a gift for watercolour painting. Vincent had five younger siblings and was closest to his brother, Theo.

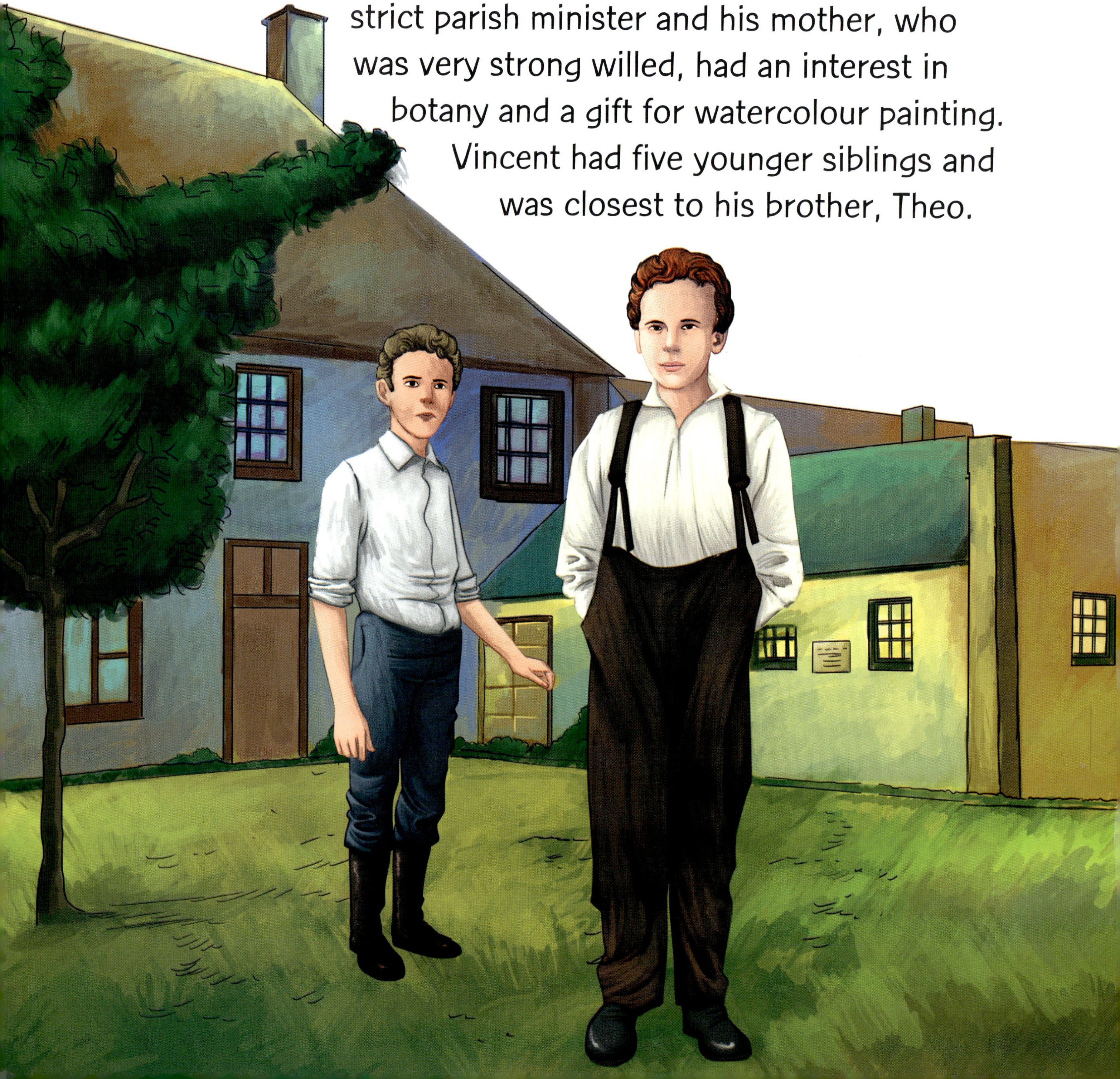

Vincent was a serious and thoughtful child who loved flowers, birds and insects. His sisters recalled him as someone who would walk clumsily in a daze, with his head hung low.

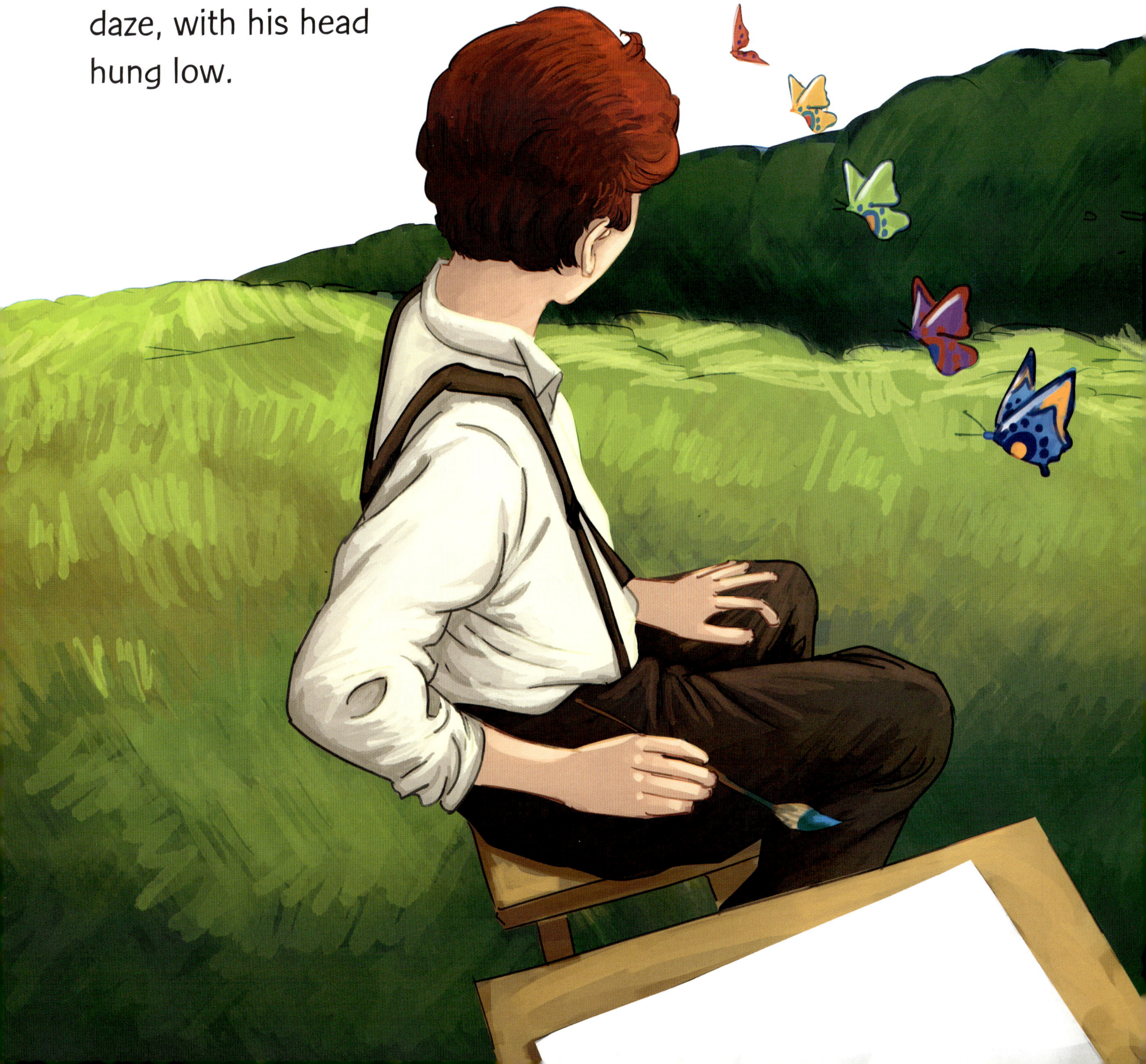

Vincent finished school in 1868 and a year later he joined his uncle's art dealership, Goupil and Cie. Based in The Hague, Vincent worked as an apprentice and an art dealer over the next few years, travelling a lot.

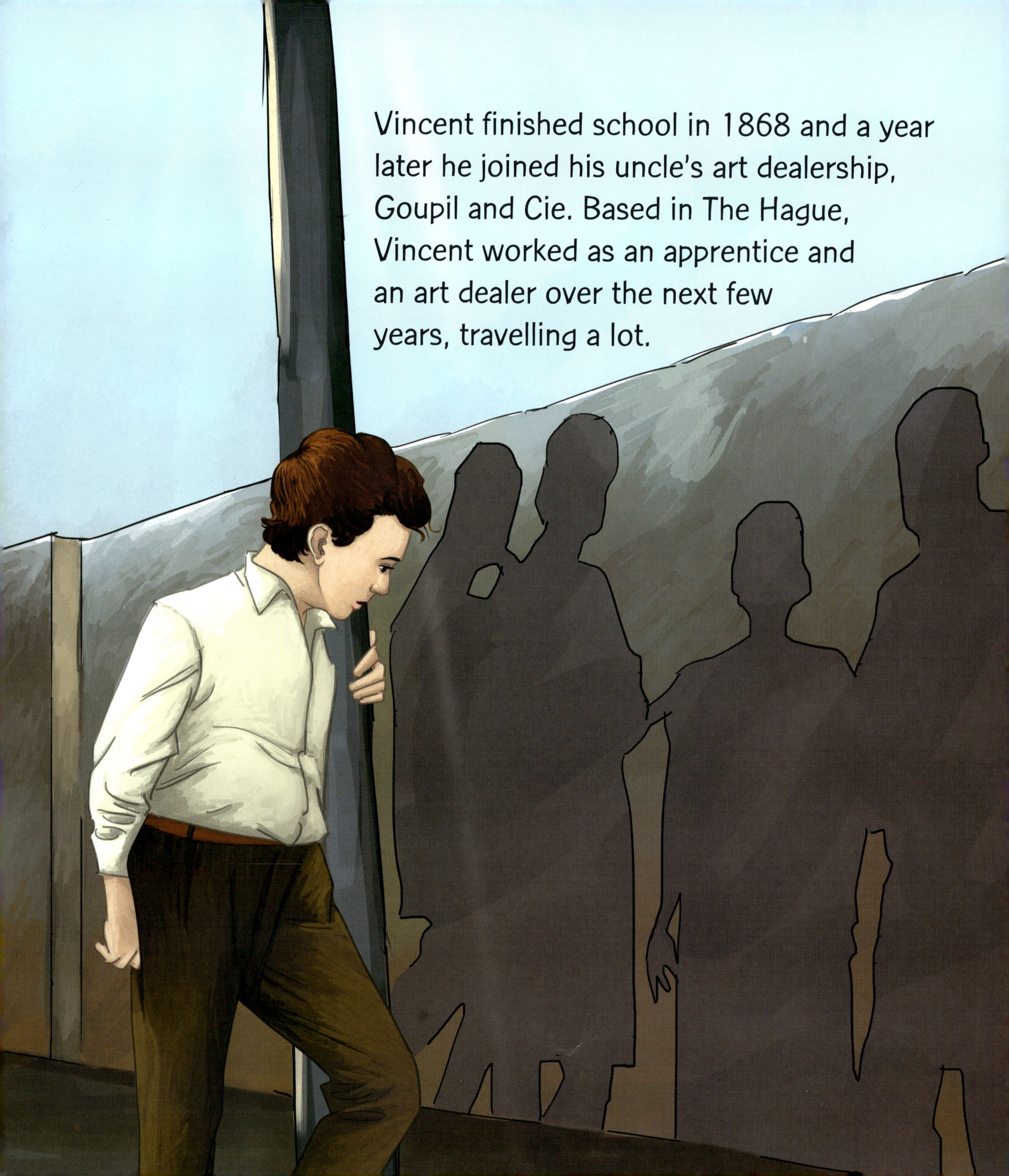

Vincent had a great memory for visual and verbal descriptions. He spoke French, German and English fluently.

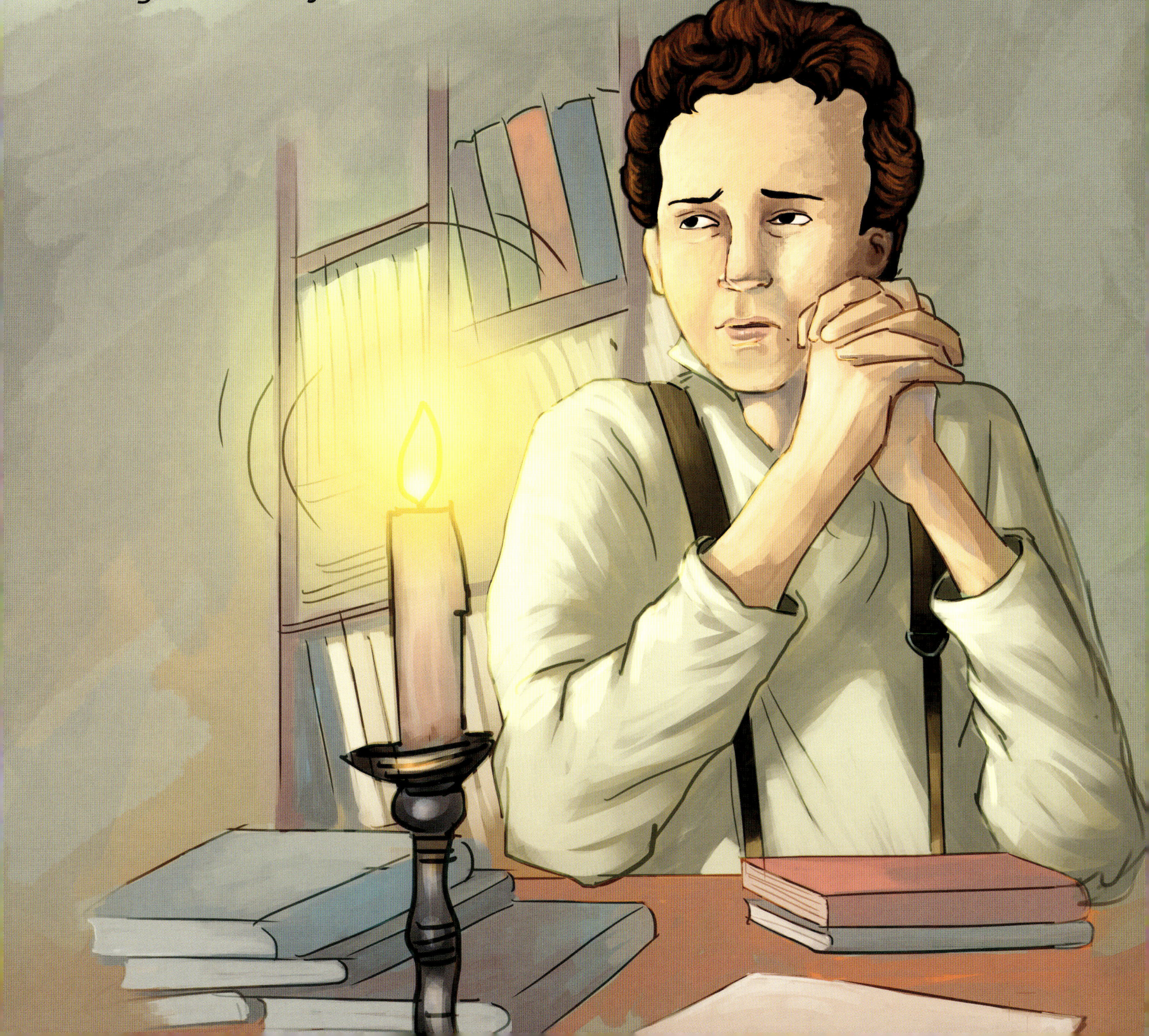

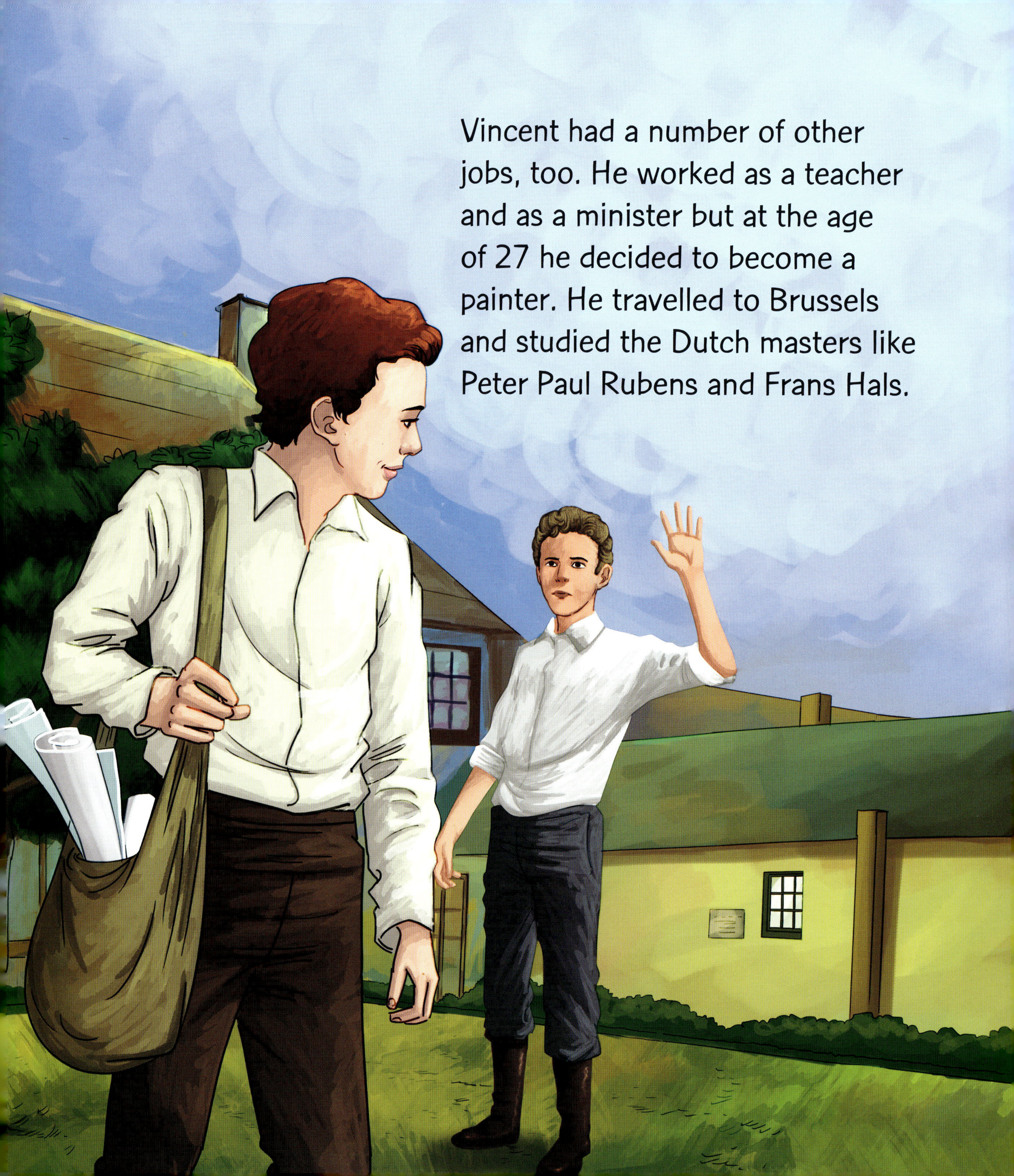

Vincent had a number of other jobs, too. He worked as a teacher and as a minister but at the age of 27 he decided to become a painter. He travelled to Brussels and studied the Dutch masters like Peter Paul Rubens and Frans Hals.

He began signing his paintings as 'Vincent', just like Rembrandt, who also signed his paintings using only his Christian name.

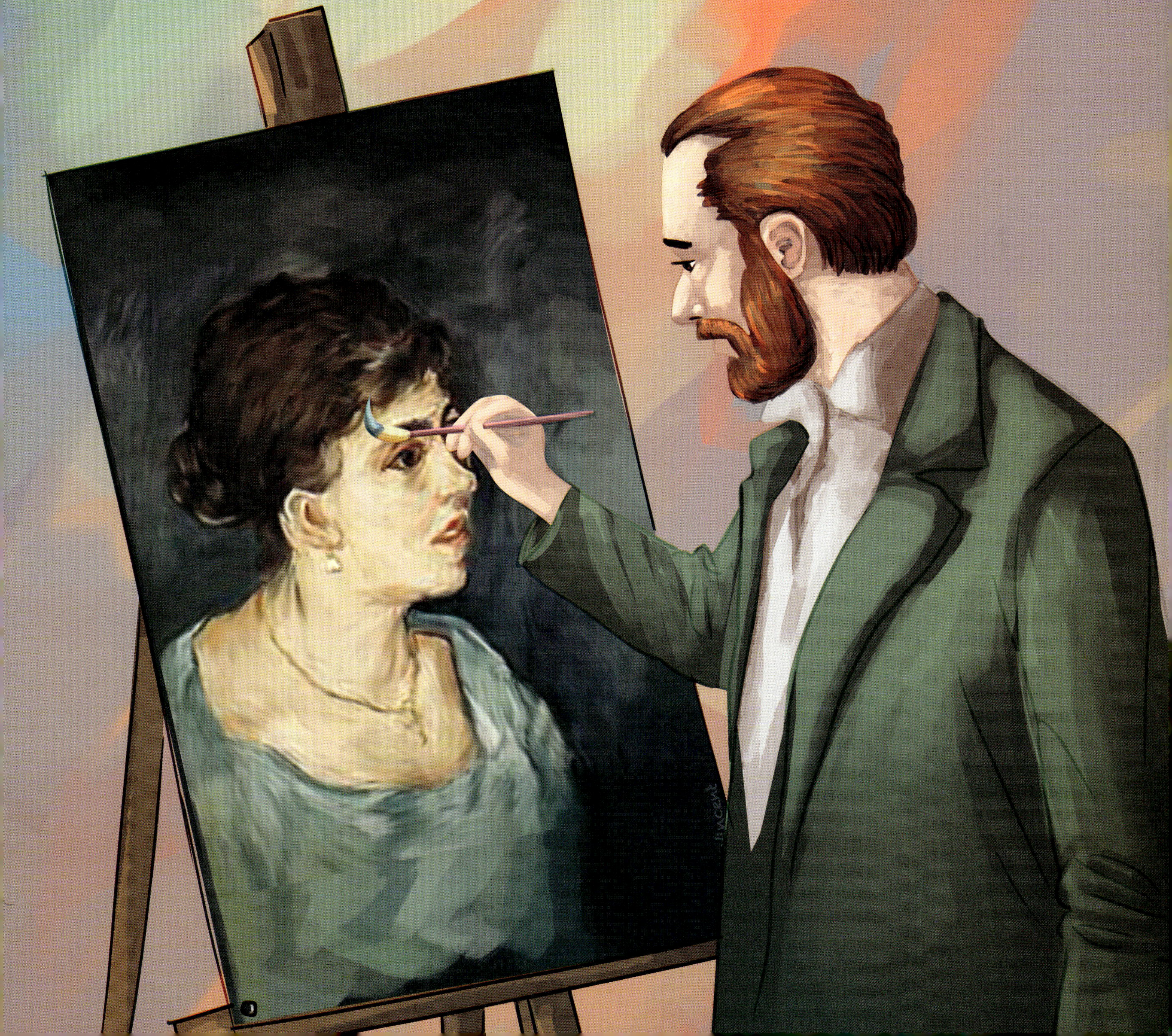

Vincent travelled to Paris to learn more about the Impressionists. He also studied newer painting styles like Pointillism. The influence of his studies showed in Vincent's paintings. He made friends with the passionate artist, Paul Gauguin.

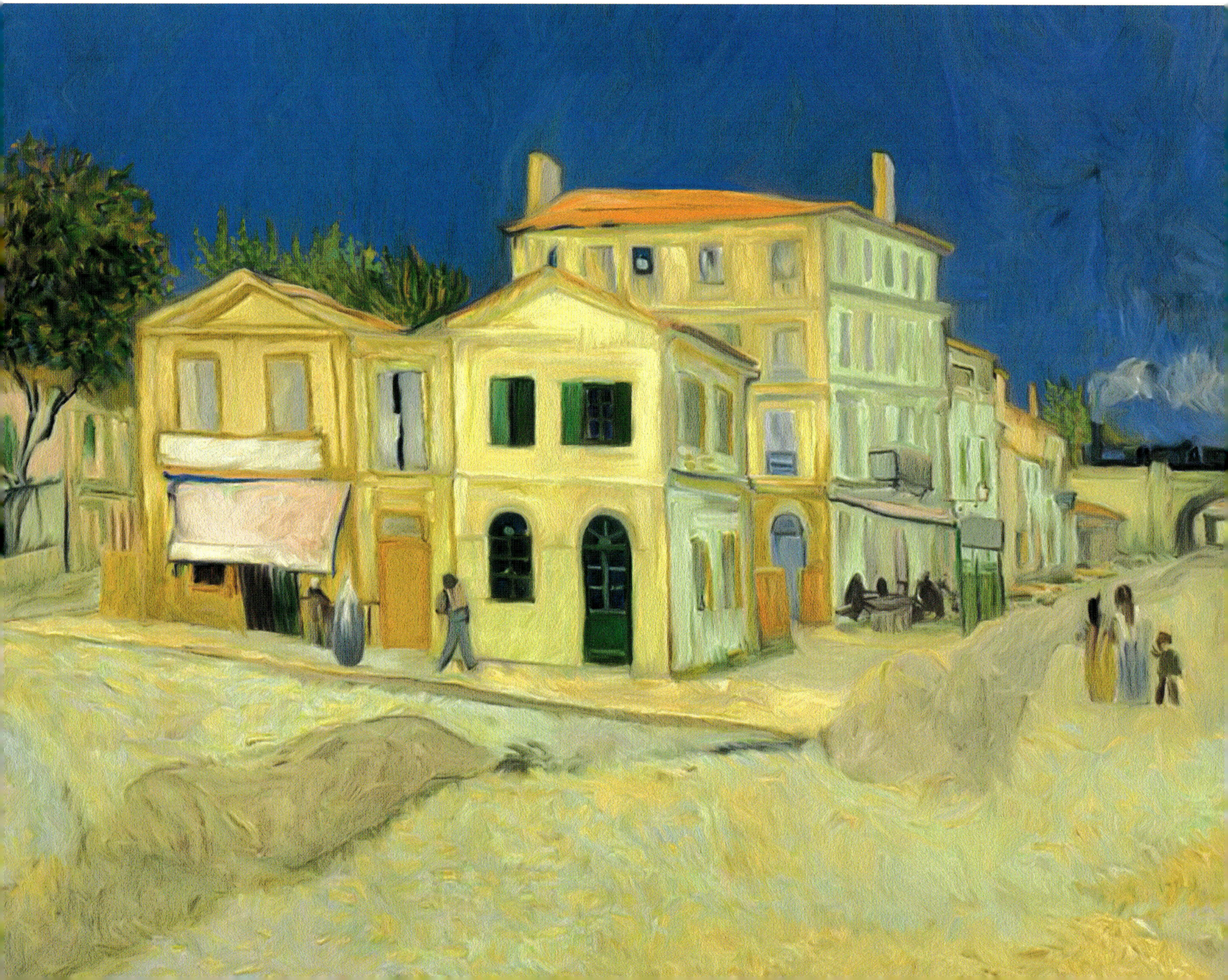

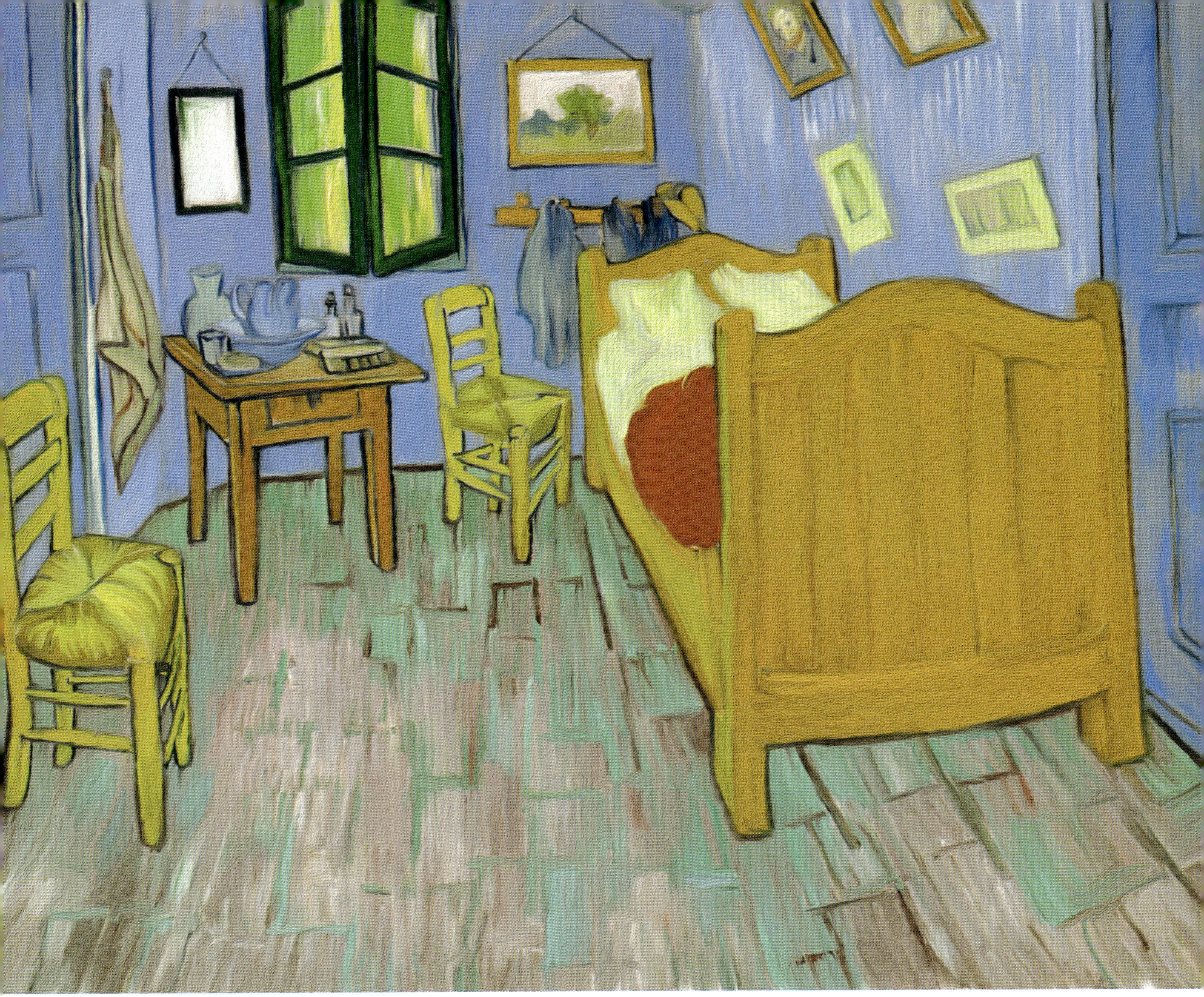

Vincent was unhappy in Paris and moved to Arles when he was 35 years old. Once there, he moved into a rickety building he called the 'Yellow House', which he painted numerous times.

After a few months, Paul Gauguin joined him in the 'Yellow House'. However, the two were very different from each other and their friendship ended when Vincent injured himself badly in 1889. After this incident, Vincent voluntarily checked into a hospital near Arles to be treated for serious mental illness.

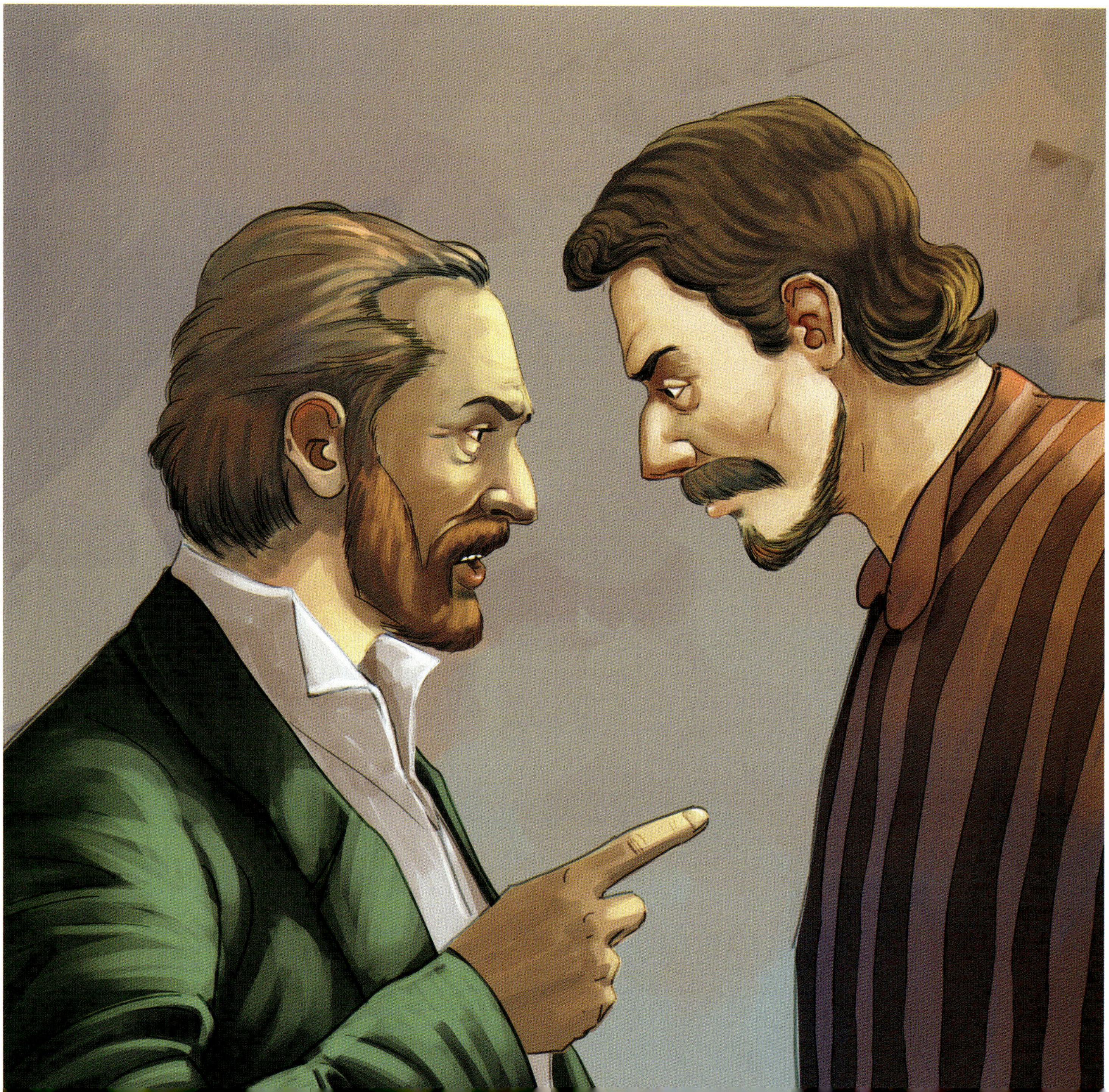

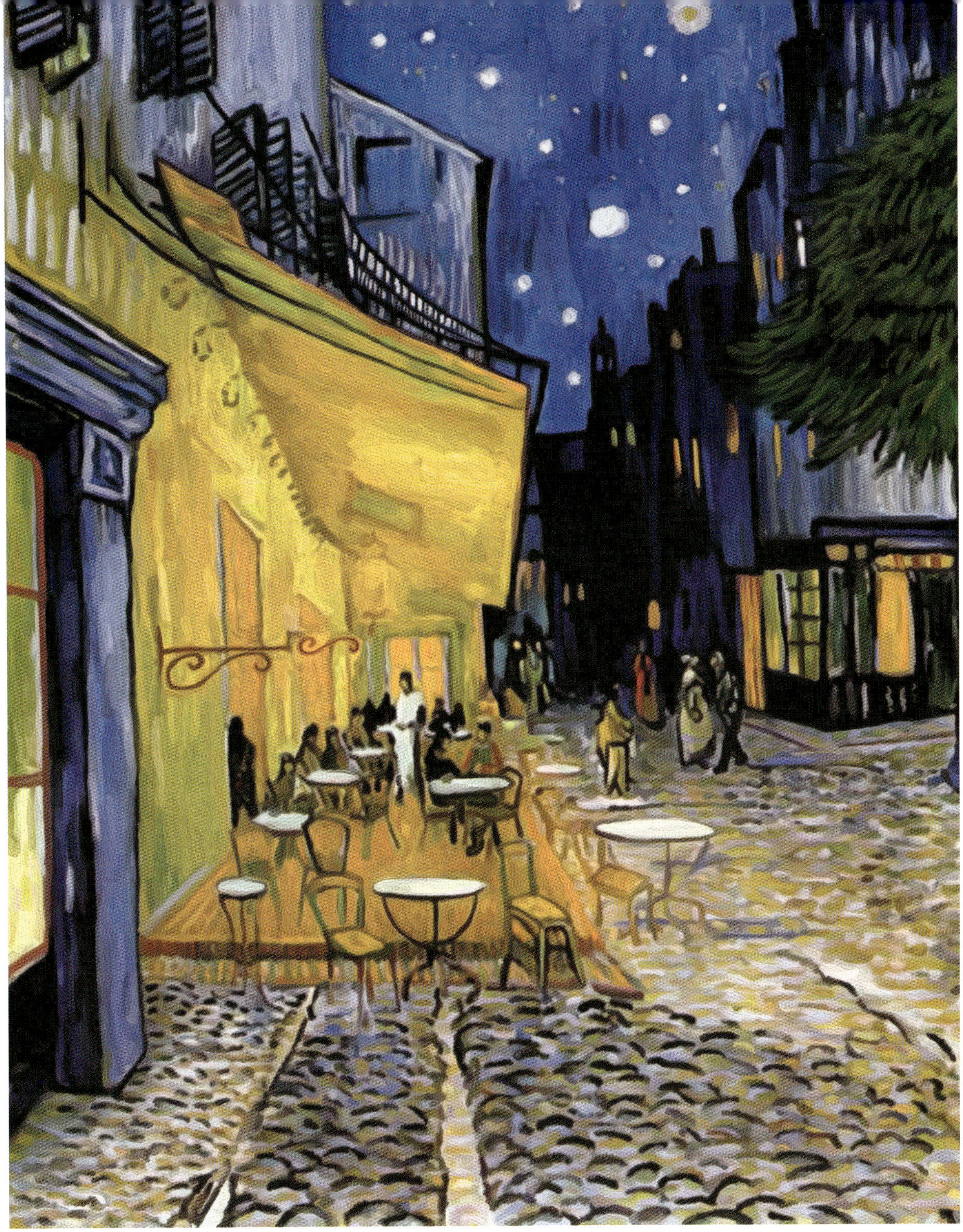

While in Arles, Vincent's paintings became more energetic and confused than ever before. One of his masterpieces from this time was the *Café Terrace at Night*.

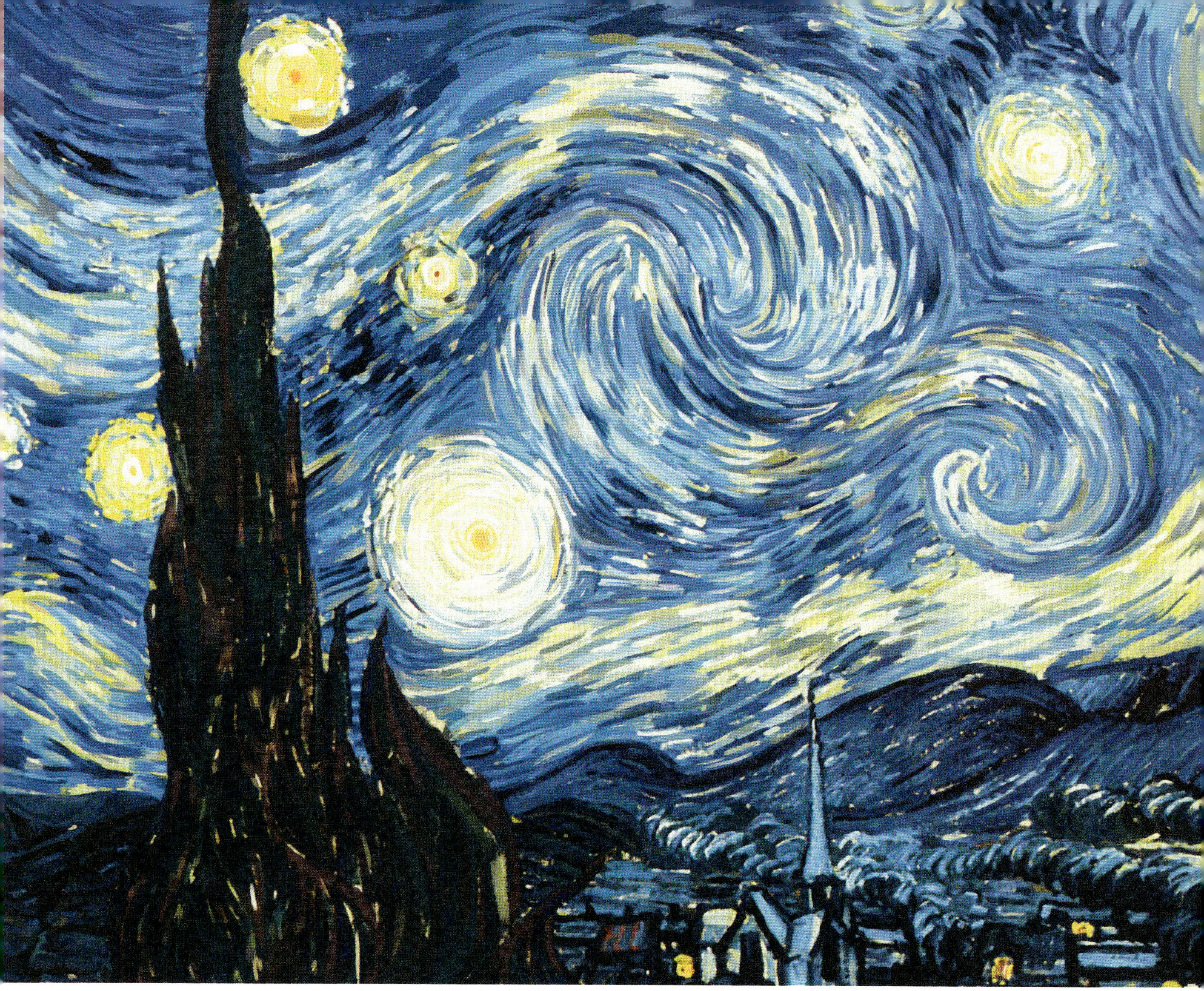

Vincent's love for vibrant colours and the atmosphere of Arles made his paintings very intense. He would even apply colours directly from the tube and use rough brushstrokes. His paintings sometimes took weeks to dry due to the thickness of the layers of paint.

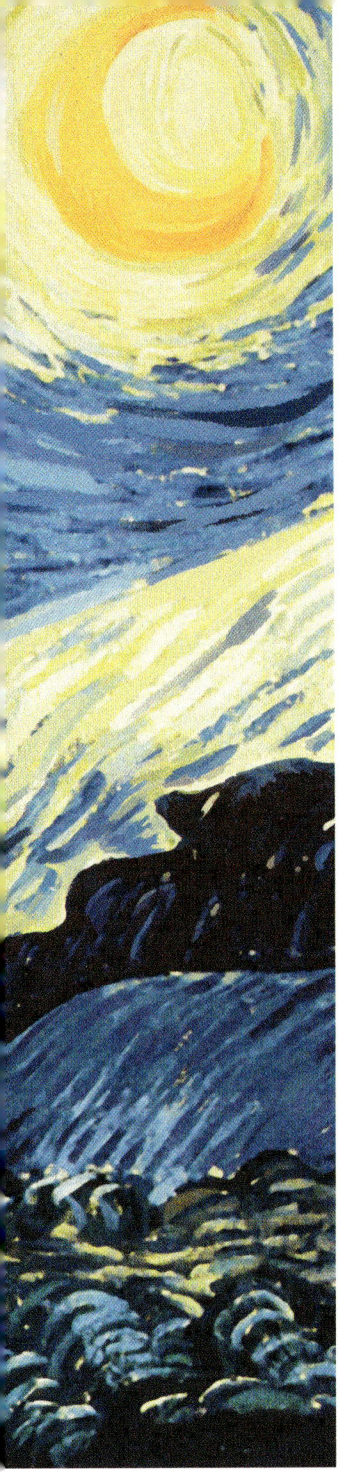

Theo tried to sell Vincent's paintings, but was unable to. In fact, he only made one major sale of Vincent's art during his lifetime – a painting called *The Red Vineyard.*

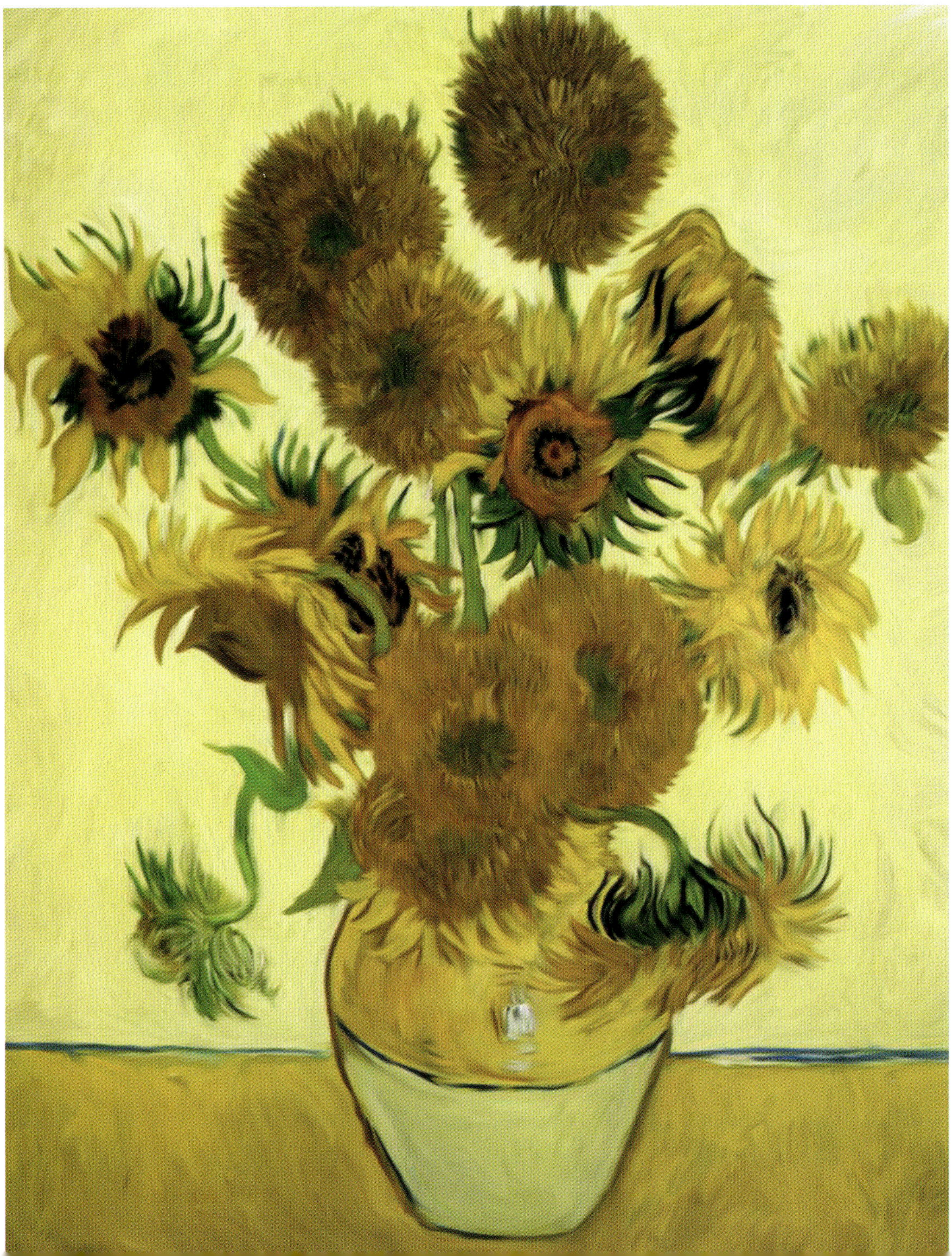

Vincent often wrote to Theo about his constant sense of loneliness. Over 600 letters exchanged between the brothers still exist today. Most of what we know about their lives is taken from these letters.

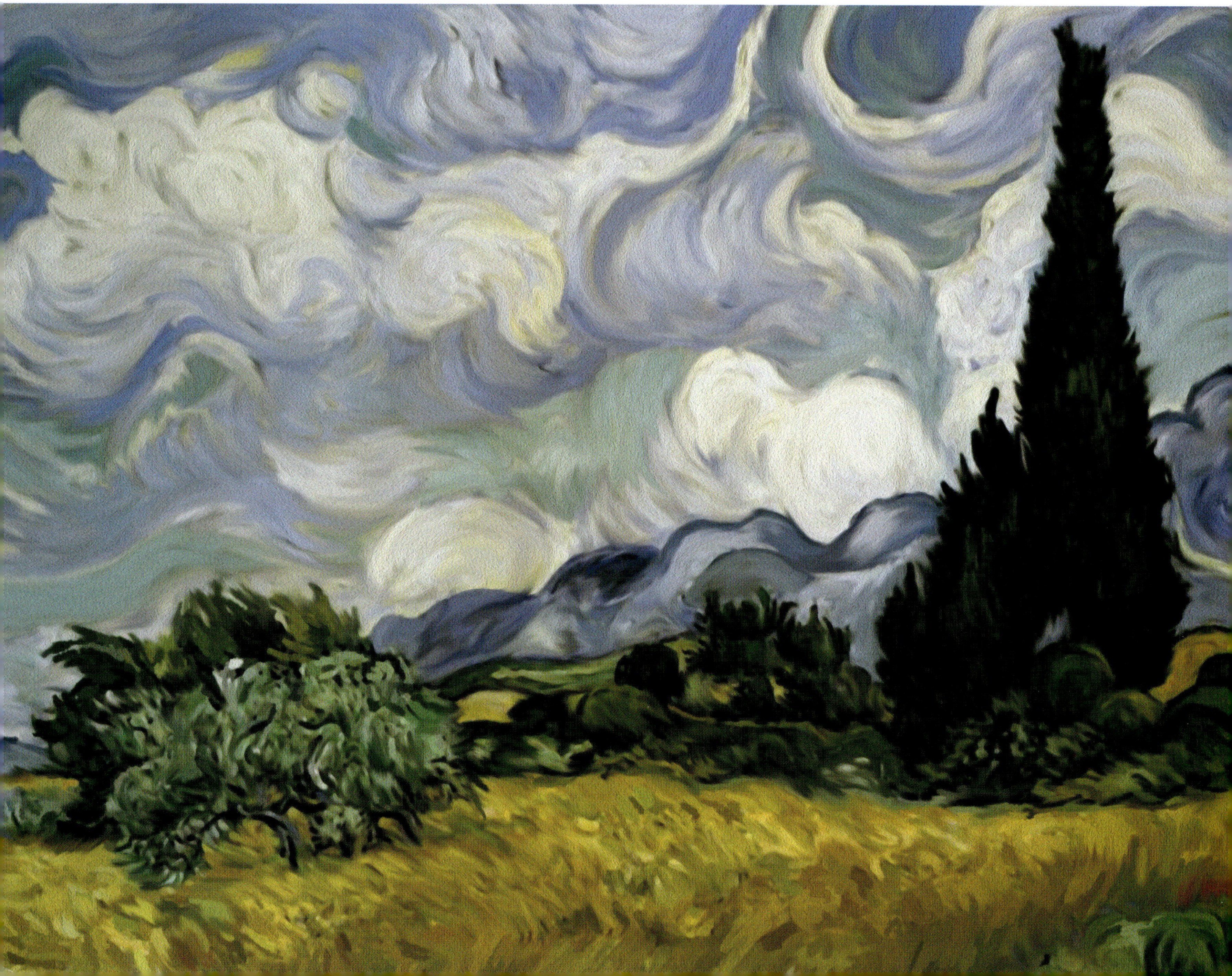

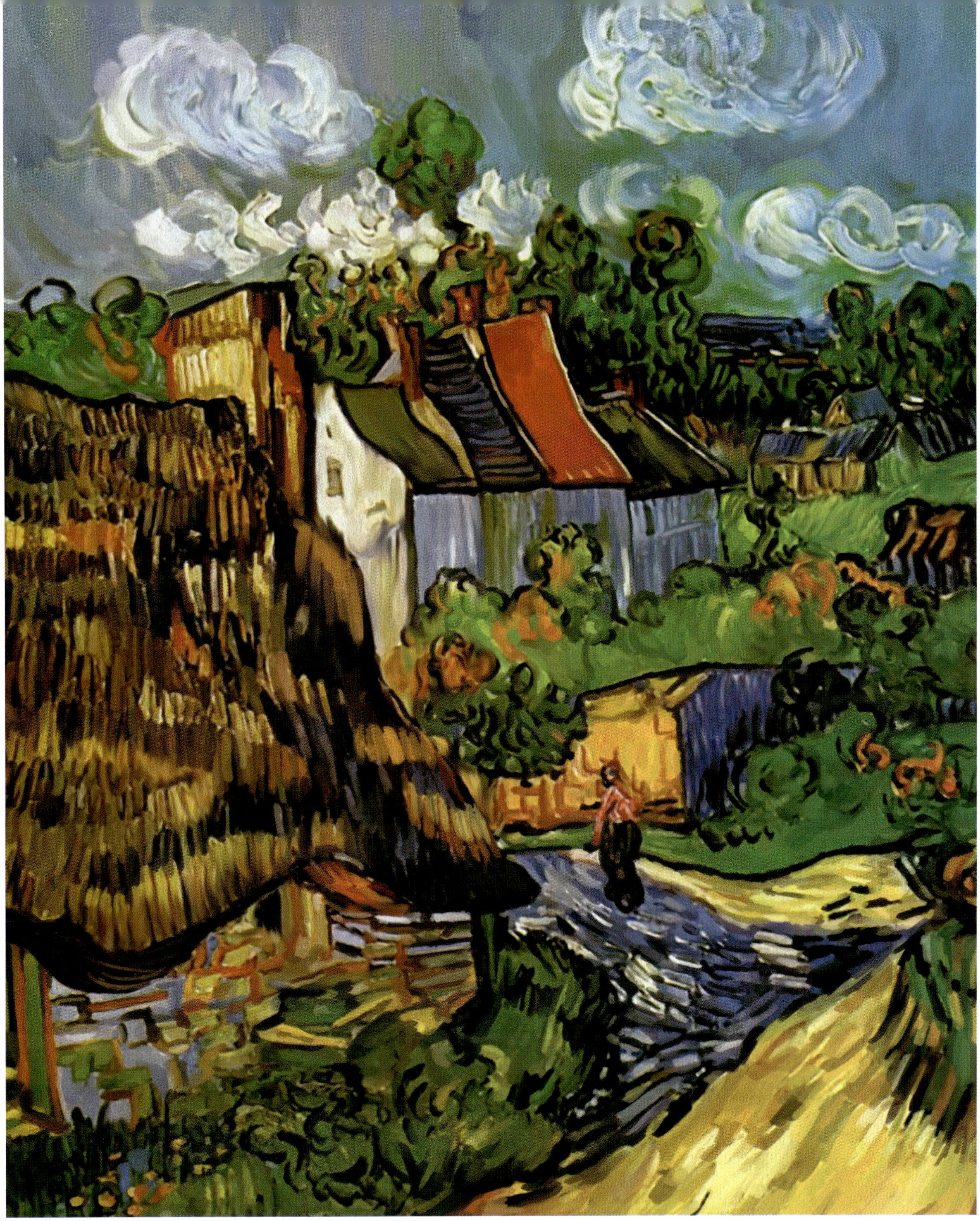

One day, when Vincent went out to paint, he sadly shot himself. He died in Theo's arms on 29 July, 1890, at the age of 37.

Although he wasn't famous during his lifetime, Vincent van Gogh is now considered to be one of the world's greatest and most influential artists of his era. His painting, *The Starry Night*, has become one of the most celebrated modern art pieces of all time.

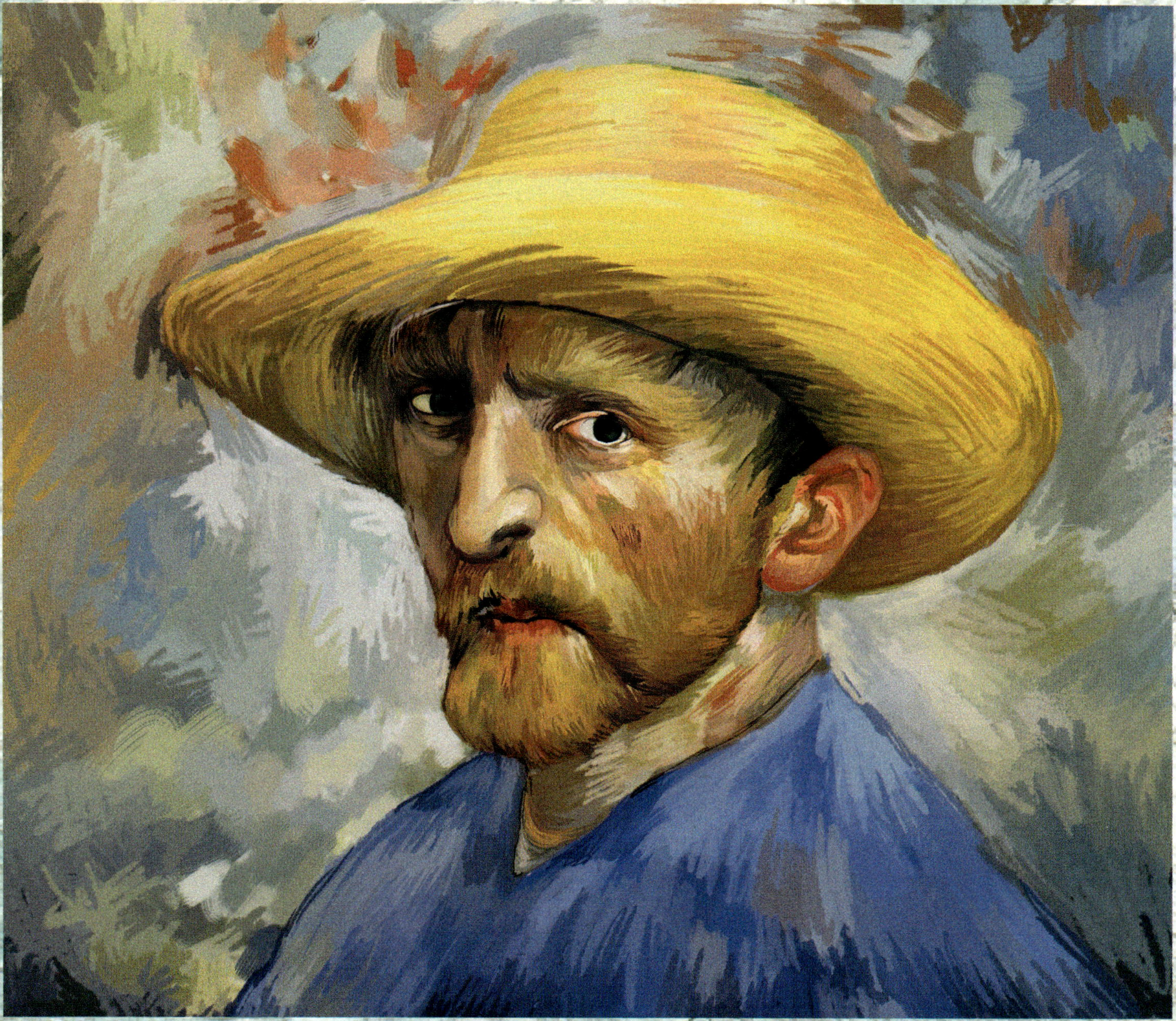